Castles and Knights

LONDON, NEW YORK, MUNICH,
MELBOURNE, and DELHI

Written and edited by Fleur Star
Designed by Jacqueline Gooden,
Laura Roberts
Publishing manager Susan Leonard
Managing art editor Clare Shedden
Jacket design Bob Warner
Jacket editor Carrie Love
Jacket copywriter Adam Powley
Picture researcher Liz Moorel
Production Luca Bazzoli
DTP designer Almudena Díaz
Consultant Christopher Gravett

REVISED EDITION
DK UK
Senior editor Caroline Stamps
Senior art editor Rachael Grady
US editor Margaret Parrish
Jacket editor Manisha Majithia
Jacket designer Natasha Rees
Jacket design development manager
Sophia M. Tampakopoulos Turner
Producer (print production) Mary Slater
Producers (pre-production)
Francesca Wardell, Rachel Ng
Publisher Andrew Macintyre

DK INDIA
Senior editor Shatarupa Chaudhuri
Senior art editor Rajnish Kashyap
Assistant editor Neha Chaudhary
Art editor Isha Nagar
Managing editor Alka Thakur Hazarika
Managing art editor Romi Chakraborty
DTP designer Dheeraj Singh
Picture researcher Sumedha Chopra

First American Edition, 2005
This American Edition, 2014
Published in the United States by DK Publishing
4th floor, 345 Hudson Street
New York, New York 10014
13 14 15 16 17 10 9 8 7 6 5 4 3 2 1
001—196173—02/2014

DK books are available at special discounts when purchased in bulk for
sales promotions, premiums, fund-raising, or educational use. For details,
contact: DK Publishing Special Markets, 345 Hudson Street, New York,
New York 10014 or SpecialSales@dk.com.

Color reproduction by Scanhouse, Malaysia
Printed and bound in China by Hung Hing

Discover more at
www.dk.com

Contents

What is a castle?

There are hundreds of amazing castles all over the world. They were more than just homes for important people, such as kings and lords—they were also defense posts against enemies. The earliest castles were built more than 1,200 years ago. Some still stand today.

Forts first

Forts, such as this one in Mycenae, Greece, existed long before castles. Like castles, they were used for defense, but while an army could sleep there, they were never used as homes.

The crenellations at the top of a castle are sometimes called battlements.

Most windows were small to stop attackers from climbing through.

Stone towers were much stronger than early wooden ones.

A typical castle?

Bodiam Castle, in southern England, was started in 1385. It has many defense features to stop enemy attackers, such as a very wide moat that is difficult to cross.

Tools used hundreds of years ago look much the same as those we use today.

Chisel

Calipers

Sledgehammer

In the loop

Most castles have lots of loopholes that soldiers could shoot arrows through. The narrow slit made it harder for the enemy outside to shoot arrows back.

This French painting shows castle building in the 1400s.

Construction site

A lord needed permission from the king or ruler to build a castle. He would get a master mason to design and build the castle, a job that took many years and many teams of workers.

The small, tall tower was a lookout post.

Castle words

Castle A fortified home for a lord or king.

Crenellations The up-and-down stonework on top of the castle.

Master mason The person in charge of designing and building a castle.

Early castles

Castle building really got going in Europe in the 11th century. Some castles were simple, wooden buildings with a fence and ditch around them for protection. The next step up, motte and bailey castles, had a big advantage: height.

High sight

A motte was an important part of castle defense. By piling up soil and building the castle tower on top, people inside could see an attacking army coming a long way off.

The wooden fence, called a palisade, was later made of stone.

A drawbridge could be raised to stop attackers from climbing up to the motte.

The soil taken for the motte left a ditch, which was an extra defense.

When William the Conqueror invaded England in 1066,

From wood to stone

The earliest stone castle was built more than 1,000 years ago in northern France— before many wooden castles. Stone castles were not popular at first because they took more time and money to build.

Looks like a good spot

Castles were built in the best places to fight off the enemy. But often, the castle builders were not the first people to use the site. These ruins at Portchester Castle, England, lie within the remains of a Roman fort.

Low life

Down on the ground was the bailey, or courtyard, where animals were kept. Staff based here could run up the wooden bridge to the tower when the enemy came near.

A typical bailey would contain stables, a hall, workshops, and a chapel.

The bridge across the moat could be lifted to stop unwelcome visitors.

he built two wooden castles in two weeks!

A castle grows

In 1077, William the Conqueror started work on a stone keep by the Thames River in London that became known as the Tower of London. More walls were added in the 13th century, and it has been changing ever since.

William the Conqueror ruled England from 1066.

The tower was the first thing seen when arriving in London by boat.

The White Tower

William's stone keep took over 20 years to build. Once used as a residence, it became a storehouse for weapons, jewels, and even prisoners!

The tower is 90 ft (28 m) high—three times as tall as its neighbors in the Middle Ages.

Outer curtain wall

The inner curtain wall has 12 towers.

Murky moat

In 1275, King Edward I added a 160-ft- (50-m-) wide moat. It took six years to build but was drained in 1830 because the water was foul. Human bones were found at the bottom when it was emptied.

This area would have been filled with water.

This is the Tower in the year 1200. The walls behind and at the top right are the old Roman walls that once surrounded the city of London.

The outer curtain wall and the moat were both in place by 1300. It was now a concentric castle, because it had a double wall.

Today's Tower has many more buildings, including offices and barracks, but others, such as the Great Hall, are gone.

Who lived there?

During the later Middle Ages, from the 10th to the 16th centuries, kings and lords lived in castles. Their servants slept in the castle, too, but the farming peasants lived in huts.

Ladies had female servants and nurses to bring up their children.

Lady of the manor
A lady would marry very young, usually around the age of 12. She gave all she owned to her husband.

The lady took care of important guests.

Lord of the manor
In addition to running his estate and being a judge, the lord's job was to be part of an army and go to war.

The apprentice
The squire was the lord's attendant, and he trained to become a knight.

A new page
Noble-born sons were sent away to other castles to become pages.

Squires started training around the age of 13.

Lords grew rich from winning wars and tournaments.

A page became a squire when he grew up.

Lady

Lord

Squire

Page

Behind closed doors

Early castles were not pleasant to live in. The only heating in the large rooms came from open fires, so it was cold and drafty. Aside from the lord, only the chaplain was important enough to have his own bedroom.

Chaplain's room

Upper hall

Chapel

Stair turret

Kitchen

Lower hall

Down on the farm

Most peasants worked in the lord's fields, growing food for the lord. He sold any spare crops to make money.

The peasants' huts were in the fields and were owned by the lord.

Castle staff

The lord had lots of staff. Some were important officials, like the constable who took care of the castle when the lord was away. The more basic tasks were done by servants, such as cooks and weavers.

Spinsters spun wool so it could be used to make clothes.

Carpenters made household objects and repaired the castle.

Carpenter

Spinster

Peasant

Food, glorious food

The great hall was a castle's main room. Here the lord would eat, entertain guests, and conduct business. At first, the whole household slept in the hall, but by about the 13th century, the lord and his family had their own bedrooms.

A feast of fun

The lord's family would enjoy a large evening meal. When they had guests, there would be a full banquet, with jugglers and minstrels.

This is the Great Hall of Warwick Castle, England.

These three doors lead to the kitchens.

Only rooms on the upper stories would have had large windows.

Some floors were tiled. Carpets were rare and had to be imported.

In the kitchen

Large castles usually had more than one kitchen. Food was kept in a pantry and cooked in the kitchen. Drinks were stored in a buttery, which was named after the butts, or barrels, that held the drinks.

Pigeon was often eaten, along with beef, pheasant, and venison.

All the food would be grown or caught on the lord's estates.

Cooking pot

Cooking tools

While knives and spoons have not changed for centuries, some utensils are very different today. Scary-looking flesh hooks were used to lift meat out of the pot, which was hung over a fire.

Flesh hook

Sauces were used to cover up the taste of bad meat.

Dinner is served

The main meal was eaten in the late morning. Meat and fish were the central dishes. Dessert was a luxury. The food was eaten off bread "plates," called trenchers.

Drink it up

In the Middle Ages, water was so foul that you could not drink it. An alewife made ale for the staff. The lord and his guests were more important, so they had wine, which was more expensive.

Time out

In the Middle Ages, there were no weekends! Peasants only had time off to go to church on Sundays and fairs on feast days. But lords and ladies had plenty of time to relax.

The sound of music

Most people could not read, so listening to music was educational as well as fun. Minstrels sang songs about war, love, and religion.

Playing the fool

The job of a jester, or fool, was to make his lord laugh. He wore a silly costume with jingling bells and told jokes.

Instruments of the time included pipes, trumpets, drums, and strings.

Lutes came to Europe from Arabia.

The entertainers

On a feast day or religious holy day, such as Easter, musicians and actors would tell the story of the festival at a village fair.

Time for prayers

Castles had their own chapels, which the lord, his family, and the castle staff had to attend daily. The lord employed a chaplain, who could read and taught lessons from the Bible.

What's the catch?

Hunting, especially with birds, was a daytime activity for the whole family. Anything caught would be eaten for supper.

Dicing with danger

Men used to play with dice as a gambling game. Some people enjoyed it so much they lost fortunes.

Dice were made of wood or bone.

Your move

Playing games was one way of passing long evenings. Chess, backgammon, and checkers were popular—and still are today.

Chess pieces represent the different classes in society, from the king down to pawns.

Bishop   Knight   King

Under siege

Living in a castle wasn't easy. Other lords wanted your land, and foreign invaders might need to capture your castle before they could conquer the country. There was a constant threat of being under siege.

Sling

Dung

Large rock

What is a siege?

The enemy would raid a village and surround its castle. They set up camp and waited... and waited... until either the lord surrendered, or he died of starvation inside. If things took too long, they attacked.

... and shoot!

This massive crossbow machine is called a ballista. It was aimed at people, and one of these outside the castle gates would stop defenders from coming out.

This shows where the bolt sits.

The bolt shoots forward when the bow is released.

Whoosh Whoosh

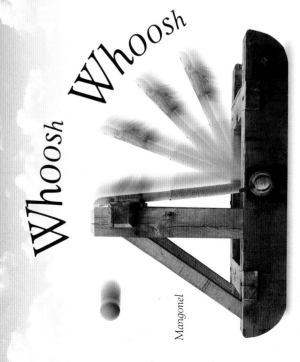

Mangonel

Ready, aim...

It was difficult to attack the high castle walls, but catapults such as the mangonel and trebuchet helped. They were used to fling rocks over the battlements.

All-purpose

Broadhead

Bodkin

Arrowheads

The archers on the ground used different types of arrow in their longbows. A broadhead was used for killing animals, while a bodkin could pierce armor.

Not all sieges came to a bloody end: the lord would often surrender.

Trebuchet

Means of attack

In addition to hand weapons and machines, the attackers used a variety of sneaky ways to get into the castle. These included climbing up drains and even bribing the guards!

Tricks of defense

The attack has started, and the enemy is at the gate. The small garrison, or army, inside the castle is up on the battlements. Can they stop the enemy from getting in?

Unwelcome visitors could end up trapped inside the gatehouse below the murder holes.

Up inside the top of the arch were the murder holes. Soldiers poured boiling liquid onto the enemy through these.

Shut the gate!

A gatehouse protected a castle's entrance. It usually had at least one heavy portcullis gate, which was lowered to cover the wooden doors behind. Some gatehouses had a defended area in front, which was called a barbican.

In hot water!
Contrary to popular belief, boiling oil was rarely used as a weapon, but boiling water and hot sand were often thrown over the battlements onto the enemy below.

However it lands, one spike always sticks up.

Watch your step
The garrison threw spiked metal caltrops on the ground to injure the feet of enemy soldiers or horses who stood on them.

Around and around...
Spiral staircases inside a castle usually turned to the right. This meant that an attacker going up had little room to swing his sword— but a defender coming down had plenty.

Hideout
Crenellations were made to hide behind. Soldiers took cover behind the higher walls and peered out to shoot arrows over the lower parts.

Soldiers dropped objects through these holes, called machicolations.

Crenellations

Lock 'em up

Castle towers were the ideal place to lock up prisoners, because they were strong buildings that were hard to break out of. Nobles who were captured in war were imprisoned so they could be held for ransom.

This collar weighs about 35 lb (16 kg). Heavy!

The collar locks around a person's neck.

No escape
Nobles held for ransom were kept in good conditions. Other prisoners were chained up as punishment, and to stop them from escaping.

Behind bars
People caught misbehaving in the Middle Ages would usually face a fine or execution. Those "inside" were political or church prisoners or criminals awaiting trial.

The cuff would fit around a prisoner's ankle.

A royal pain
It was common to torture prisoners, sometimes with instruments. In England you had to get a license from the king or queen to torture prisoners.

A tongue-puller

HISTORY MYSTERY
Edward V was just 12 years old when he became king in 1483. His uncle Richard locked him and his brother in the Tower of London, supposedly for their own protection. Richard then claimed the throne for himself, and the boys disappeared... 200 years later, workmen found bones in the tower. Had he murdered them?

A long stretch

Many "confessions" were given under torture. Before the rack was invented, some prisoners were tied between two horses and pulled apart. Others were forced to stand in burning hay.

Vaults would often have neck or leg chains secured to the posts.

Many prisoners died in a castle's dungeons.

Where am I?

Not every castle had a prison. Those without one would keep their prisoners in any spare room. In 1553, Bishop Latimer was kept in a henhouse at the Tower of London!

The knight

Kings and dukes needed armies to defend their lands. It was the lord's job to serve his ruler by being a knight—a professional soldier who fought on horseback.

Plate armor was the knight's best defense against weapons.

It was important to protect the horse in battle.

A team of horses

A knight had to have his own armor and a horse. Some even had five horses: for war, hunting, jousting, traveling, and carrying baggage.

Women warriors

While only men could be knights, ladies were expected to defend their husband's castle. Some even went to war—including nuns!

In 1429, Joan of Arc tried to save the French king by leading an army into battle.

A bed for the knight

Not all knights had their own land. Some lived in another lord's castle as part of his garrison. The lord paid for their costly armor.

The lord

Samurai were famous for their archery skills with bows 6½ ft (2 m) long.

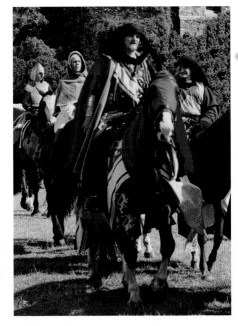

Follow the leader

A knight employed staff who followed him into battle. They helped him mount and dismount his horse, and took care of the horses and weapons.

Samurai were the ruling class of Japan until the 16th century.

Knight or not?

Japanese warriors were not knights; they were Samurai. They lived by their own rules, called *bushido*, which means "the way of the warrior."

Knight school

A lord had to go through training to become a knight. Work started early: at around seven years old, a lord's son would leave home to work as a page. This led to being a squire.

Are you being served?

Both pages and squires served the lord's family at dinner. Squires would do the more impressive jobs, such as carving meat. Pages might pour the drinks.

Practice makes perfect

Learning to ride horses and control weapons was vital. Aiming a lance at a target was a common way of training.

Even trained knights kept practicing.

The wooden board swings around when it is hit.

No pain, no gain

A page became a squire at about the age of 13. The lord then trained him to be a knight. He had to learn how to fight and use weapons, which included wrestling and throwing javelins. He would be dubbed, or made a knight, around the age of 21.

The lord wore an arming doublet under his armor.

Best behavior

Knights had to behave in a certain way, which was called chivalry. It started out as rules for battle, but soon spread to everyday life.

First lessons

A page was taught manners by the lady of the castle. Only some were taught to read.

Chivalry rules included how to treat ladies.

It only took about 15 minutes to put on all the armor.

Dress to impress

The squire was the lord's personal servant. He dressed the lord in armor, took care of his weapons, and went everywhere with him—even into battle.

25

All wrapped up

The first thing that comes to mind when you think of a knight is his armor. No other horseback warriors in the world had armor that looked quite like the plate armor of the European knights.

Chin up
The bevor protected the face and throat. The name comes from an Old French word that means "to dribble."

Underarm protection
A besagew was more than a fancy plate: it provided extra defense by covering a gap, or chink. If chinks were left uncovered, weapons could get through them.

Besagew

The couter did not bend, but the knight could move his arm inside it.

The gauntlet had a leather glove inside.

The average sword was 30 in (75 cm) long—as long as the knight's leg!

Symbolic sword

A knight's sword and spurs were given to him when he was dubbed. If these were taken away from him, it meant he was no longer a knight.

The knight used sharp spurs to control his horse.

The top of the cuisse, or thigh plate, strapped on to the body.

The poleyn, or knee-covering, connected to the cuisse.

The greave over the shin was one of the first parts to put on.

The sabaton was a series of plates that moved when the knight walked.

He's wearing a skirt!

There were no plates to cover the knight between the cuisse and the breastplate. Instead, he wore a skirt made of mail. It was flexible, so the knight could sit down.

Armor words

● **Chink** A gap in the armor where the plates meet.

● **Couter** A solid plate that covers the elbow.

● **Dubbing** The ceremony when a squire became a knight.

● **Mail** A kind of armor made of iron links.

27

In shining armor

Soldiers have always needed protective clothing. The earliest types of armor were padded clothes and a mail jacket. Over time, weapons became stronger, and so did the armor.

Poleax

Armor basics

A suit of plate armor weighs around 55 lb (25 kg), about the same as a seven-year-old child. It is made in sections, or plates, so it is quite easy to walk in, but very hot to wear.

Mail to plate

Mail is flexible armor made from iron rings linked together. It gave little protection against swords; hard steel plates were better.

Italian armor made in 1380

Coming in the mail

The Bayeux Tapestry shows the Norman invasion of England in 1066. The knights are wearing mail coats and a coif, or hood made of mail, with a helmet on top.

On your head

During the 14th century, coifs were replaced by helmets with mail attached at the bottom. Many later helmets had no mail.

Italian helmet for warfare

Close-helmet for tournaments

Open-face helmet for parades

The height of fashion

Later armor, especially that used for parades and tournaments, was based on local fashions. It could take six men to make just one suit.

German armor made in 1500

English armor made in 1587

HEAVY KNIGHTS

It's a myth that armor was so heavy that the knight had to be lifted onto his horse with a crane. But he did need attendants to pick him up if he fell off his horse in battle and was hurt. They also cleaned his armor with a mixture of sand and urine to stop it from getting rusty.

Weapons of war

A knight was called on to fight battles over land ownership and who was ruler. It was not common to have large wars during the Middle Ages: a ruler could lose a whole army this way.

Mane protection

Warhorses were so valuable in battle that some were given armor. The most popular kind was a caparison, a cloth "skirt."

Soldiers had to follow rules of how to act in battle.

War hammer

Glaive

Mace

Close combat

Many weapons were mounted on long wooden staffs, or poles. Maces were shorter, which shows how closely the two sides fought.

Length of service

One of the few major wars of the Middle Ages was between France and England. It was called the Hundred Years' War, but it lasted 116 years, from 1337 to 1453!

Into battle

Knights made up only a part of an army. Foot soldiers protected them before they charged. During the 14th century, many knights dismounted and fought alongside the foot soldiers.

The army charged with staff weapons until they were close enough to use a mace or sword.

Joust for fun

The knights of the Middle Ages were more than soldiers—they were also the sports stars of the time! When not in battle, they entertained crowds with tournaments, which were also good practice for fighting.

Horseplay

Early tournaments had one event: a fight between teams of knights on horses. Other events were added later, so this one was renamed the tourney.

This knight has just broken his lance, so he has lost the joust.

How to play

Jousting was a high-speed skill. A knight had to knock his opponent off his horse using a lance. The victor could win lots of prize money.

The tilt, or fence, stops the horses from charging into each other.

On the defensive

Each knight had his own shield to use in combat. This one was used during the joust—its curved edge supported a lance. The shield was important for defense.

A lance would fit neatly into this gap.

Not playing fair

● In early times, many knights were killed at tournaments.

● King Edward I banned tournaments because the knights were jousting instead of going to battle for him.

The handle was solid wood, for balance.

Lance

Lances for jousting were hollowed out so they were not too heavy.

Choose your weapon

Early tournaments used sharp battle weapons. Later on, most weapons were blunted so the knights were not killed— but they could still be injured.

The mace could seriously damage armor.

Mace

When upright, the ax is as tall as an adult.

Poleax

Helmets were padded inside to protect the head.

Foot combat

Early foot tournaments saw two knights battling each other. This changed to whole teams fighting across a barrier. Prizes for these events were smaller.

Tournaments could have three events: the tourney, jousting, and foot combat.

Heraldry

Noble families each had a "coat of arms"—their own special symbol that was like having their own logo. Knowing who someone is from their coat of arms is called heraldry.

Early signs

One of the first coats of arms is shown on the tomb of Geoffrey Plantagenet; it dates back to 1160.

Geoffrey was Duke of Normandy, an important French nobleman.

Shield

When a knight was dressed in armor, it was hard to see who he was. So knights displayed their family coats of arms on their shields.

The pommel, or end of the sword, is shaped like a lion's head.

Presenting arms

● A knight would only ever have one coat of arms.

● Arms were passed down from father to son. If there was more than one son, the others would change the symbols.

● Arms are unique: no other person would have the same.

Every new coat of arms had to be registered.

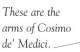

These are the arms of Cosimo de' Medici.

Just for show

This sword belonged to the 16th-century Italian nobleman Cosimo de' Medici, the Duke of Florence. His arms show that he belonged to an order of knights.

What does it mean?

Heraldry has its own language, based on Old French, to describe the colors and patterns on arms. There is also a secret meaning behind the background color and symbols used.

Gules (red)

Vert (green)

A lion means a generous spirit, and red is the color of a warrior.

A dog means loyalty, and a silver background is peace.

If arms are quartered, it shows two families that have joined together in marriage.

A unicorn shows courage and purity, and green is hope and joy.

An owl means vigilance and wit, and a blue background is truth.

Argent (silver)

Azure (blue)

Coat of arms on a pottery jar dating from around 1500

This ring prints its owner's coat of arms when it is pressed into a wax seal.

A good impression

Arms were originally a status symbol of upper-class families. But after knights displayed them, the rest of society caught on. Even towns would have their own arms.

The Crusades

In 1096, Christian Europeans went to the Middle East to fight the Saracens—Muslim warriors who were taking over the land. The nine wars that followed over the next 200 years were known as the Crusades.

How it began

The Christian emperor of Byzantium asked Pope Urban II to help with defense against the Saracens. He gave a speech to the rulers of Europe and persuaded them to go to war.

The People's Crusade

It wasn't only knights who supported the Pope. Peasants, women, and children went off on their own People's Crusade. They were unsuccessful, but the knights reclaimed Jerusalem in the First Crusade—for a while.

This 16th-century picture of the Crusades shows the knights in 16th-century armor.

What's in a name?

● "Saracen" was the European name for all Muslims. Muslims called the Europeans "Franks."

● Alexius I was emperor of Byzantium, where Greece and Turkey are today.

In addition to hospitals, the Knights of St. John built castles. The biggest is Krak des Chevaliers in Syria.

Call to order

Many Crusader knights signed up to military orders. The two most famous are the Knights Templar and the Knights of St. John, who were also called the Knights Hospitaller because they cared for the sick.

This is the seal of the Knights Templar. The motto reads "The Seal of the Order of Christ."

The other side

The Crusaders fought against the Saracens, who fought on horseback, used curved swords, and carried round shields.

Following orders

After the Crusades, kings created their own orders so that knights would be loyal to them. By the 16th century, there were lots of new orders, including the Order of the Garter, whose symbol is a cross of St. George.

Shopping trip

Europeans traveling to the Middle East saw a different world. They brought back exotic fruit, cotton clothes, and even sugar—before the 12th century, they used honey instead.

Sugar

Cotton

Dates

Moorish castles

The Moors were Arabs who came to Europe from north Africa. They brought with them a different type of castle design, with domes, arches, decorative walls, and water features.

The four towers are called Square, Round, Tribute, and Crumb.

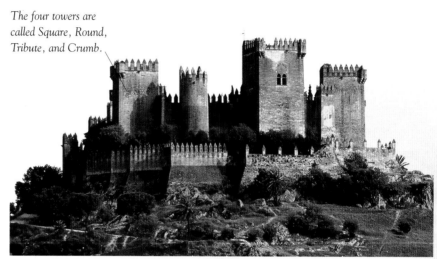

Moor information

● The Moors ruled over large parts of Spain and Portugal in the Middle Ages.

● In 1492, the Catholic rulers of northern Spain drove the Moors out of southern Spain.

● The Spanish rulers captured the Alhambra and lived there.

The castle by the river

The Almodóvar del Rio, in Córdoba, Spain, has a network of underground tunnels, dungeons, and water wells. It was important to have a store of water in case of a siege.

No one knows for sure how old this kasbah is, but it was probably built in the 16th century.

Movie star

One of the most famous Arab castles, called kasbahs, is found in Ait Benhaddou in Morocco. Its style is so typical that it has featured in many Hollywood movies.

Writing on the wall

Walls and ceilings inside Moorish castles are decorated in an Arabic style. They feature patterns of brightly colored tiles and verses from the Koran, the Islamic holy book.

Al-hamra means "the red one." The fort's walls glow red at sunset.

This door is in one of the Alhambra's royal palaces, where Moorish kings lived.

This part of a royal palace is called the Tower of Hens.

Enemies could be seen through the small gaps in the fort's walls.

Fantastic feat

It took more than 140 years, from 1298, to build the Alhambra, in Granada, Spain. The oldest part is the fort, to which three royal palaces and an estate of cottages and gardens were added.

Asian castles

With their own unique styles, Japanese, Chinese, and Indian castles are different not only from those in Europe, but also from one another.

A truly ancient castle
Yumbulagang Castle was built in the 1st century BCE. Its Tibetan name means "the palace of mother and son," because it has two parts.

The Sun's castle
Mehrangarh, in India, takes its name from *Mehr*, which means "Sun." Its walls are 120 ft (37 m) high and 20 ft (6 m) thick. No wonder it has never been captured!

Chinese emperors lived here from 1420 to 1911.

Passage turrets connect the large tower to the three smaller ones.

Castle city
China's Imperial Palace in Beijing is actually a whole fortified city that was finished in 1420. It was also called "The Forbidden City" because commoners were not allowed to enter.

Himeji castle

Japan's biggest castle, Himeji, was first built as a fort in 1346 and has been rebuilt twice. It is composed of 83 buildings. The tower, shown here, was started in 1601.

The five-story tower actually has seven levels inside.

A cool coat

Although the tower is stone, its frame and interior are wood. The outside is covered in plaster to make it fireproof.

Himeji is also called "White Heron Castle" because of its white walls.

Towering strengths

With their massive height and thick walls, towers are a castle's key defense. Although they were harder to build, round towers were better than square towers—but towers come in all shapes and sizes.

This is a typical medieval château, with a drawbridge, moat, and towers.

French châteaux

The Loire Valley, France, is famous for its castles, or châteaux. They have a special French design of narrow towers with high roofs.

It took 44 years to build Château de Chaumont, from 1466 to 1510.

The unusually shaped towers are called "pepper pots."

The 500-year-old drawbridge still works. It leads to a courtyard.

I like your style

Different castle styles depend on when and where they were built. Twelfth-century Gothic castles are tall and imposing, but 15th-century Renaissance castles are more ornate.

German Gothic

Some German castles, such as the Gothic-style Burg Eltz, have strange shapes. Built on mountains or crags, they had to fit in the smallest of spaces.

Welsh walls

Conwy Castle in Wales is built into the town walls. The castle has eight round towers, and there are another 13 in the town walls. They are over 70 ft (20 m) tall.

A plan of the castle from above

Pieces of eight

The unique Castel del Monte in Italy has octagonal towers around an eight-sided keep. It was built by Frederick II in 1249 as a hunting lodge.

Swedish style

The town of Kalmar, Sweden, grew up around its 12th-century castle. The castle was rebuilt in 1540 in the Renaissance style, with decorative towers.

Castles today

Imagine living in a castle! In the Middle Ages, they were cold and uncomfortable places to live. Later castles were grander, with more luxuries. Even now, people build houses to look like castles as a sign of power and wealth.

The house on the hill

Casa Loma, which means "the house on the hill," was built by Sir Henry Pellant between 1911 and 1914 in Toronto, Canada. However, Sir Henry could not afford to pay for it, so he ended up living on a farm.

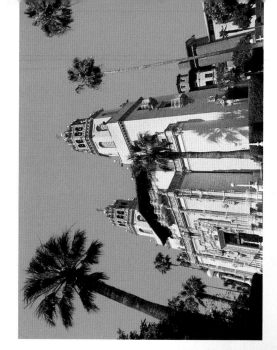

Bed and breakfast

If you want to live in a castle, you could stay in one on vacation. Some old castles are now hotels, and some new hotels look like romantic old castles.

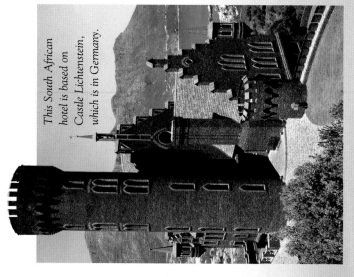

This South African hotel is based on Castle Lichtenstein, which is in Germany.

American dream

Between 1919 and 1947, in California, William Randolph Hearst built himself a castle... and three guest houses, a zoo, swimming pools, and tennis courts!

King Ludwig II wanted the castle to look like "the old German knights' castles."

It's a fairy tale
Walt Disney used Neuschwanstein as a model for Cinderella's castle in Walt Disney World, Florida.

Fit for a king
King Ludwig II of Bavaria wanted Neuschwanstein Castle to be his dream home. Work started in 1869. It was so ornate it took 14 carpenters four years to do the carvings in his bedroom alone!

True or false?

It's time to test your knowledge of castles and knights. Can you spot which of these statements are true and which are false?

Italian helmets were worn for tournaments.
See page 29

At Easter, **musicians and actors** would tell the Easter story at village fairs.
See page 14

Hunting was a daytime activity for the whole family.
See page 15

A suit of **plate armor** could weigh more than 220 lb (100 kg).
See page 28

To win a **joust**, a knight had to knock his opponent off his horse.
See page 32

As well as being used for defense, **forts** were homes for important people.
See page 4

It was very common to torture prisoners, sometimes with **instruments**.
See page 20

A **unicorn** stands for a generous spirit, and green is the color of a warrior.
See page 35

A **lady** of the manor would get married around the age of 20.
See page 10

A **page** was a nobleman's son who was sent away to other castles.
See page 10

Conwy Castle in Wales is built into the town's walls.
See page 43

Facts matchup

How much do you know about castles and knights? Each of these things can be found in the book—read the clues and see if you can find the correct answers among the pictures.

Joan of Arc

Collar

Metal caltrops

Sabaton

Spinster

Glaive

Peasant

He made household objects and repaired the castle. **See page 11**

This was used for killing animals. **See page 17**

He wore a silly costume with jingling bells and told jokes. **See page 14**

This castle in Italy was built by Frederick II in 1249 as a hunting lodge. **See page 43**

This was placed around a prisoner's ankle to stop him from escaping. **See page 20**

She spun wool so it could be used to make clothes. **See page 11**

If under attack, a garrison might throw these on the ground to injure the feet of their enemies. **See page 19**

Neuschwanstein Castle

Broadhead

Castel del Monte

Lance

Ballista

Cuff

Carpenter

Jester

Dice

Château de Chambord

Walt Disney used this castle as a model for Cinderella's castle in Walt Disney World, Florida. **See page 45**

These were made of wood or bone and used in gambling. **See page 15**

This weighed about 35 lb (16 kg) and was locked around a prisoner's neck. **See page 20**

She tried to save the French king by leading an army into battle. **See page 23**

Part of a knight's armor, it covered the foot and was made of a series of plates that moved when the knight walked. **See page 27**

This weapon was mounted on a long wooden staff, or pole. **See page 30**

It took 44 years to build this castle. Its towers are called "pepper pots." **See page 42**

This hollow weapon with a wooden handle was used in jousting tournaments. **See page 33**

He worked in the lord's fields, growing food for the lord. He sold any spare crops to make money. **See page 11**

This massive crossbow machine was used to throw bolts and spears at people. **See page 16**

What's this?

Take a look at these close-ups of things in the book and see if you can identify them. The clues should help you!

🗡 This war was fought between France and England.

🗡 It lasted 116 years, from 1337 to 1453.

See page 31

🗡 This protected a castle's entrance.

🗡 It was lowered to cover the wooden doors behind.

See page 18

🗡 This is Japan's biggest castle.

🗡 It is also called "White Heron Castle" because of its white walls.

See page 41

🗡 This musical instrument was used in the Middle Ages.

🗡 It came to Europe from Arabia.

See page 14

🗡 This castle is located in India.

🗡 Its walls are 120 ft (37 m) high and 20 ft (6 m) wide.

See page 40

- It is a Moorish castle.
- Its walls and ceilings feature patterns of brightly colored tiles.

See page 39

- These replaced coifs during the 14th century.
- This piece of armor had mail attached at the bottom.

See page 29

- This is a symbol for a military order created after the Crusades.
- It represents the cross of St. George.

See page 37

- This tower is 90 ft (28 m) high.
- It was once the first thing to be seen if arriving in London by boat.

See page 8

- This piece of armor was worn by warhorses.
- It looked like a cloth "skirt"!

See page 30

- Each knight had one of these to use in combat.
- This one was used during a joust and its curved edge supported a lance.

See page 33

A knightly quest!

A knight's job is to protect the king. But he has lost his way. Help him find the way to the king's castle. Let's see who wins!

Run away from a dung attack. **Go back 4**

Find a route map. **Move forward 3**

Clean your rusty armor. **Skip a turn**

How to play

This game is for up to four players.

Move down   **Move up**

You will need

A die

Counters—one for each player

Trace over the helmet outlines or cut and color your own from cardboard. Each player takes turns throwing the die and begins from the START box. Follow the squares with each roll of the die. If you land on an instruction, make sure you do as it says. Good luck!

Ask the page for directions. **Move forward 3**

Stop and listen to the minstrels. **Skip a turn**

START

52

FINISH
Congratulations! The knight has reached the castle!

Find an open drawbridge.
Move forward 2

Pray at a chapel.
Skip a turn

Ride a horse to move faster.
Move forward 3

Fight intruders.
Go back 5

Oops! You fell into a deep pit.
Go back 5

Look out for the spiked caltrops!
Go back 3

Eat fruits to get energy.
Move forward 2

53

Glossary

Here are the meanings of some words that are useful to know when learning about castles and knights.

arming doublet A jacket worn under armor with mail attached to fill the gaps in the plates.

bailey The courtyard of a castle that had workshops or other buildings inside. Animals were also kept here.

ballista A giant crossbow on wheels that shot massive bolts.

barbican Part of the defenses on the outside of the castle walls. It usually protected the gate.

battlements The stonework on top of a castle with gaps for soldiers to shoot weapons through. Also called crenellations.

besagew The part of a suit of plate armor that covered the armpit.

bevor The part of a suit of plate armor that covered the neck and chin.

caltrop A four-pointed, spiked weapon thrown on the ground to injure horses and foot soldiers.

chaplain The man who led prayers in the chapel and taught lessons from the Bible to the family.

chivalry The knights' code of conduct—how they should behave in war and in love.

coif An early type of mail armor that covered the head.

concentric castle A castle with two walls around the outside.

couter The part of a suit of plate armor that covered the elbow.

crenellations Another name for battlements on top of a castle.

crossbow A bow with a wooden handle that shot short arrows called bolts.

cuisse The part of a suit of plate armor that covered the thigh.

dubbing The ceremony where a squire became a knight. He was tapped on the neck or shoulder with a sword.

feudal system The class system of the early Middle Ages in Europe. The king was at the top and owned all the land. Bishops and barons were below him, then the lesser lords, and finally the peasants. Feudalism died out by the 1600s.

fort A strong building or set of buildings that protected defenders. People did not live in a fort.

garrison A group of soldiers who lived in the castle.

gauntlet The part of a suit of plate armor that covered the hand, like a metal glove.

glaive A weapon with a long blade on the end of a pole.

great tower The main tower of a castle. It usually contained a hall, the lord's rooms, and storerooms.

greave The part of a suit of plate armor that covered the shin.

heraldry Use of coats of arms to identify knights and noble families.

joust A competition between two knights on horseback. They used lances to knock their opponent off his horse.

keep Another name for the great tower of a castle.

lance A long wooden pole with a pointed metal tip, used as a weapon.

longbow A large and powerful bow used to shoot arrows.

loophole A narrow opening in a wall that soldiers could shoot weapons through.

lord Any nobleman who was also a knight. Most lords owned castles and had staff working for them.

mace A club with a heavy metal end that could crush armor.

mail A type of armor made of metal rings linked together.

mangonel A catapult that was used to throw stones at a castle during a siege.

master mason A man who designed castles. He would be trained in stonework.

minstrel A poet who sang and played instruments. He entertained at castle feasts.

moat A ditch around a castle, often filled with water.

motte A natural or human-made mound in a castle, on which stood a wall and often a tower.

page A young son of a noble family who was sent to another castle to serve the lord and start training to be a knight.

palisade A wooden fence around a castle used for defense.

peasant A lower-class person who worked the lord's lands.

plate armor A suit of armor made up of metal plates.

poleyn The part of a suit of plate armor that covered the knee.

portcullis A heavy grille that was lowered to protect the castle entrance against enemies.

ringwork An early type of castle that had banks of earth and a wooden fence for defense.

sabaton The part of a suit of plate armor that covered the foot.

siege When the enemy surrounded and attacked a castle to force its lord to surrender.

squire A young nobleman who was a page and now is the lord's servant and a knight in training.

tournament Display of fighting skills by knights and squires, which included jousting.

trebuchet A tall catapult used during a siege.

war hammer A hammer with a sharp point that could pierce plate armor.

Index

Acknowledgments

Dorling Kindersley would like to thank:
Cathy Chesson for design assistance; Andy Cooke for artwork; Peter Bull for digital artwork; Sarah Mills and Karl Stange for picture library services.

Picture credits

The publisher would like to thank the following for their kind permission to reproduce their photographs:
t-top, b-bottom, r-right, l-left, c-center, a-above, f-far

1 **Alamy Images**: Alasdair Ogilvie/The National Trust Photolibrary. 2 **Dorling Kindersley**: Geoff Dann/Courtesy of the Wallace Collection, London tl. 3 **Getty Images**: Photographer's Choice. 4 Corbis: Buddy Mays tl. 4-5 **Alamy Images**: Worley Design. 5 **Arcangel Images**: tl. 5 www.bridgeman.co.uk: Giraudon/Bibliotheque Sainte-Genevieve, Paris ca. 5 **Dorling Kindersley**: Geoff Dann/Courtesy of the National Guild of Stone Masons and Carvers, London tr, tcl; Torla Evans/The Museum of London tcr. 6-7 **Dorling Kindersley**: Dave Rudkin/Gordon Models - modelmaker. 7 **Corbis**: Robert Estall tr. 7 **Photo-Links.com**: cla. 8 **Corbis**: Bettmann tl. 8 **Getty Images**: Robert Harding World Imagery bl. 8-9 **Topfoto. co.uk**/English Heritage. 9 **Alamy Images**: Adrian Chinery tr. 9 The Board of Trustees of the Armouries: Ivan Lapper cra, crb, br. 10 **Alamy Images**: Liquid-Light Photography l. 10 **Topfoto.co.uk**: The British Library/HIP tl. 11 **Alamy Images**: geophotos tl. 11 **Dorling Kindersley**: Geoff Brightling/Courtesy of the Order of the Black Prince cb. 12 **Dorling Kindersley**: British Library tr. 13 **Corbis**: Ludovic Maisant cal. 13 **Dorling Kindersley**: Torla Evans/The Museum of London bc, cbr. 14 **Bodleian Library, University of Oxford**: tcr. 14 **Dorling Kindersley**: Geoff Dann/Courtesy of the Anthony Barton Collection c, bl. 14-15 A1 Pix: Superbild. 15 **Collections**: Roy Stedall-Humphreys tl. 15 **Dorling Kindersley**: Geoff Dann/The British Museum; Torla Evans/The Museum of London c. 16 **Dorling Kindersley**: Colin Keates/Courtesy of the Natural History Museum, London ca. 16 The Picture Desk: The Art Archive/JFB r. 16-17 Dick Clark. 17 Dick Clark: r. 18 **Alamy Images**: Kevin White tr. 19 **Alamy Images**: Seymour Rogansky b. 19 **Dorling Kindersley**: Geoff Dann/Courtesy of the Board of Trustees of the Royal Armouries cal. 19 **Topfoto.co.uk**: HIP/The British Library tl. 20 **Corbis**: Richard T. Nowitz cra. 21 Chateau Chillon. 21 **Corbis**: Bettmann tl. 21 **Dorling Kindersley**: Harry Taylor/Courtesy of the Natural History Museum,

London br. 22 **Dick Clark**: 23. akg-images: tc. 23 **Dick Clark**: clb. 23 **Topfoto.co.uk**: br. 24 www.bridgeman.co.uk: British Library tl. 24-25 **Dick Clark**. 25 **Dorling Kindersley**: The British Museum cl. 25 **The Picture Desk**: The Art Archive tcl. 26-27 **Corbis**: Elio Ciol. 28 **Dick Clark**: l. 29 www.bridgeman.co.uk: Musee de la Tapisserie, Bayeux, France with special authorisation of the city of Bayeux tcl. 29 **Corbis**: Philidelphia Museum of Art bl. 29 **Dorling Kindersley**: Geoff Dann/Courtesy of the Wallace Collection, London cra, bc, cal, car. 30 **Corbis**: Kit Houghton tl. 30 **Dorling Kindersley**: Geoff Dann/The British Museum bcl. 30-31 www.bridgeman.co.uk: Earl of Leicester, Holkham Hall, Norfolk tl. 32 **Dick Clark**: tl. 32-33 **Dick Clark**. 33 **Dick Clark**: br. 33 **Dorling Kindersley**: Geoff Dann/Courtesy of the Wallace Collection, London tl, a, car. 34 **Dorling Kindersley**: Geoff Dann/Courtesy of the Wallace Collection, London bc. 36 **Corbis**: Archivo Iconografico, SA tl, b. 37 **Alamy Images**: Expuesto/Nicolas Randall tr. 37 www.bridgeman.co.uk: Giraudon/Bibliotheque Nationale, Paris, France bl. 37 **Corbis**: Francis G. Mayer c; Origlia Franco/Sygma cra. 37 **Dorling Kindersley**: Angus McBride cla. 38 **Alamy Images**: LifeFile Photos Ltd/Emma Lee car; Pat Behnke bl. 38-39 **Corbis**: Hubert Stadler. 39 **Alamy Images**: Ian Dagnall tr. 39 **Corbis**: Patrick Ward tc. 40 **A1 Pix**: Superbild cra. 40 **Alamy Images**: Panorama Stock Photos Co Ltd/Hu Weibiao clb; 40 **Corbis**: Sheldan Collins cla. 40-41 **Alamy Images**: SC Photos/Dallas and John Heaton. 41 **Corbis**: Michael S. Yamashita tr. 42-43 **Alamy Images**: AM Corporation. 43 **Corbis**: Dave Bartruff bc; Massimo Listri cb; Paul Thompson/Eye Ubiquitous ca. 43 **Getty Images**: Stone/Stephen Studd tc. 44 **A1 Pix**: tl. 44 **Corbis**: ChromoSohm Inc./Joseph Sohm tr; Jose Fuste Raga bcr. 44-45 **Getty Images**: Taxi/Josef Beck. 45 **Alamy Images**: Ian Dagnall tcl. 46 **Corbis**: Buddy Mays bl. 46 **Dorling Kindersley**: The Wallace Collection, London (tl). 48 **Corbis**: Kevin Jordan (br). **Dorling Kindersley**: Board of Trustees of the Royal Armouries (cra); Order of the Black Prince (c); Warwick Castle, Warwick (cr). 49 **Dorling Kindersley**: Board of Trustees of the Royal Armouries (tc); The Wallace Collection, London (tl); Order of the Black Prince (ca). **Getty Images**: Dea / G. Dagli Orti (cb). 50 **Alamy Images**: Kevin White (cl). **The Bridgeman Art Library**: Earl of Leicester, Holkham Hall, Norfolk (tr). **Corbis**: Sheldan Collins (br). **Dorling Kindersley**: Anthony Barton Collection (bc, bc); Anthony Barton Collection (bc, bc); The Wallace Collection, London (bl). **Dorling Kindersley**: Anthony Barton Collection (bc, bc); Anthony Barton Collection (bc, bc); The Wallace Collection, London (bl). 51 **Alamy Images**: Ian Dagnall (tl). **Corbis**: Francis G. Mayer (tr); Kit Houghton (br, bl). **Dorling Kindersley**: The Wallace Collection, London (bc, tc). **Getty Images**: Robert Harding World Imagery (c). 52 **Dreamstime.com**: Tomasz Bidermann (cr). 54-55 **Getty Images**: Image Bank/Angelo Cavalli. 56 **Alamy Images**: Trevor Smithers. 56 **Dorling Kindersley**: Geoff Dann/Courtesy of The Wallace Collection, London c.

All other images © Dorling Kindersley.
For further information see: www.dkimages.com